INTRODUCTION

I congratulate you on your excellent taste in snakes—garter and ribbon snakes are, in my opinion, among the finest captives available to the contemporary herpetoculturist.

If you take the time to look at what's available commercially, you'll no doubt notice that garter and ribbon snakes are far from being the most *popular* serpents. Kingsnakes, Milk Snakes, rat snakes, Bullsnakes and their relatives, and boids (boas and pythons), all appear much more often on price lists and so forth, but that doesn't mean garter and ribbon snakes are necessarily poor pets. In fact, they are great pets. Anyone who has ever had the pleasure of keeping one will vouch for that. I would guess one reason advanced hobbyists avoid them is because they feel that would be taking a "step backwards;" garters and ribbons have, after all, earned

the somewhat unenviable reputation of being "beginner's snakes." It would be like A. J. Foyt skidding around his driveway on a Big Wheel (if anyone actually remembers that classic kid's toy).

But please, I beg you, give these wonderful snakes a second look. All of the characteristics we hold in such high regard among the more popular pet snakes can be found in garters and ribbons—they are easy to feed, house, and breed, and come in a variety of attractive colors and patterns. They are also very inexpensive and relatively well-mannered. Pretty good arguments in their favor, I'd say.

The fact is, garter and ribbon snakes *are* very popular, but only among those who are just starting out in herpetoculture (and, of course, the few advanced hobbyists who have

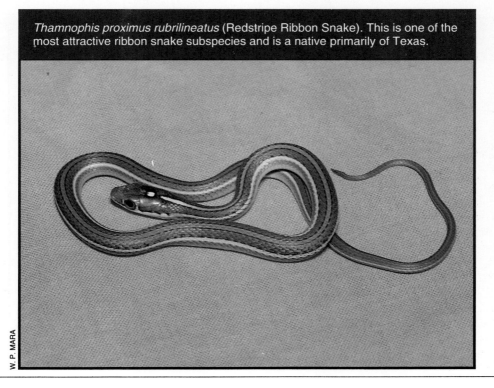

Thamnophis proximus rubrilineatus (Redstripe Ribbon Snake). This is one of the most attractive ribbon snake subspecies and is a native primarily of Texas.

W. P. MARA

a thick streak of good taste). It is a sad situation for those who have overlooked them, for I have experienced the joys of keeping garter and ribbon snakes and must say I would (and will) gladly keep them again in the future.

This little manual was written with keepers in mind, from the beginner to the pro, and will provide the interested reader with everything he or she needs to know to successfully house, feed, and even breed any garter or ribbon snake they might happen to have. It is my most sincere wish that when the reader finishes the book, he or she will then have a renewed enthusiasm for these amazing little creatures, a better grip on all aspects of their husbandry, and years of pleasure to look forward to as they confidently and skillfully lead their pets toward long, healthy, and (re)productive lives.

Good luck to you.

W. P. Mara

AUTHOR'S ACKNOWLEDGMENTS

I would like to thank Eric Thiss, Joseph T. Collins, Ernie Liner, Dr. Douglas Rossman (who is, undisputably, *the* garter and ribbon snake authority on this earth), Scott Berke, Jerry Walls, Ray Hunziker, and, in particular, Jordan Patterson, for their invaluable assistance during the production of this book. Their helpful suggestions and selfless sharing of information has made my task easier than I could ever describe.

Thamnophis sirtalis tetrataenia (San Francisco Garter Snake). This is considered one of the rarest, if not *the* rarest, snakes in the United States.

KEN LUCAS

GARTER AND RIBBON SNAKES OF THE UNITED STATES AND CANADA

SUZANNE L. AND JOSEPH T. COLLINS

Thamnophis cyrtopsis (Blackneck Garter Snake). This is an adult specimen from Catron County, New Mexico.

I had no intention of making this book incomplete in any way, but I thought when I worked up the chapter on natural history I would confine the garter and ribbon snakes discussed to those that only occurred in the United States and Canada. The reason was simple—most readers will only be able to relate to these species and subspecies anyway. Those that are found further south are rarely, if ever, offered in the pet trade, and it is my belief that a reader will be more interested in those snakes that he or she will be able to study at home rather than those that will always remain unobtainable.

K. H. SWITAK

Thamnophis sirtalis fitchi (Valley Garter Snake). The Valley Garter Snake is the most northerly ranging of all *Thamnophis*, some specimens being found in southeastern Alaska.

GEOGRAPHIC RANGE

The genus *Thamnophis* is indeed widespread; they may, in fact, be a prime example of the word, zoogeographically speaking. The most northerly ranging example, the Valley Garter Snake, *Thamnophis sirtalis fitchi*, can be found in southeastern Alaska, which is really most incredible. It speaks volumes for the amazing hardiness of the animal. Southeast of Alaska, a number of *Thamnophis* can be found in Canada, including a small population near Fort Smith in the Mackenzie District (the Red-sided Garter Snake, *Thamnophis sirtalis parietalis*). As far as the United States is concerned, it would be easier to map out where garter and ribbon snakes *don't* occur rather than where they do. There is at least one species of *Thamnophis* in every state, and, due to this phenomenon, there is, as one might imagine, a great degree of range overlap and subsequent intergradation, primarily among subspecies.

The Santa Cruz Garter Snake, *Thamnophis atratus*, occurs over

Thamnophis marcianus (Checkered Garter Snake). The Checkered Garter Snake is fairly common in the herpetocultural hobby and is primarily located in Texas.

RON EVERHART

W. P. MARA

Garter and ribbon snakes can be found in a wide variety of habitats, although almost all species will stay fairly close to water. Above, a littered pine habitat in central New Jersey. Below, a rocky, wooded hillside in Baja California.

K. H. SWITAK

much of northwestern California, then north into the southwestern corner of Oregon. The Shorthead Garter Snake, *Thamnophis brachystoma*, can be found primarily in southwestern New York and northwestern Pennsylvania, but there are a few locality reports just outside this main range that are questionable, plus there is an

around the Reno area. *Thamnophis cyrtopsis*, the Blackneck Garter Snake, one of our prettiest, is a resident of extreme southern Colorado and southeastern Utah, then extends southward over much of New Mexico and Arizona, western and central Texas, and further on into tropical Mexico. The Western Terrestrial Garter Snake,

Thamnophis ordinoides (Northwestern Garter Snake). Only being found in the northwestern corner of the United States and then north into Canada, *T. ordinoides* is a beautiful creature that is rarely, if ever, seen in captivity.

introduced population in Pittsburgh. Butler's Garter Snake, *Thamnophis butleri*, occurs over much of western Ohio, into northeastern Michigan, and central Indiana, then north into Ontario. There is also a disjunct population in Wisconsin. The Western Aquatic Garter Snake, *Thamnophis couchi*, occurs over much of northeastern California and into a small part of western Nevada

Thamnophis elegans, can be found over a large portion of the western United States and well into western Canada. The Mexican Garter Snake, *Thamnophis eques*, occurs primarily in, as you could have guessed, Mexico, but reaches into the United States in southeastern Arizona and just barely into southwestern New Mexico. The Giant Garter Snake, *Thamnophis gigas*, is only known

JOHN IVERSON

Thamnophis sirtalis parietalis (Red-sided Garter Snake). Ranging over most of central North America, there is, most interestingly, a melanistic population of this subspecies in central Montana.

Baja. *Thamnophis marcianus*, the Checkered Garter Snake (known at one time as Marcy's Garter Snake), is primarily found in Texas, with surrounding populations in Oklahoma, Kansas, Colorado, New Mexico, Arizona, California, and then into Baja and south from Texas into Mexico. The Northwestern Garter Snake, *Thamnophis ordinoides*, occurs only in the northwestern corner of the country—extreme northwestern California, western Oregon and Washington —then into the extreme southwestern corner of British Columbia and onto Vancouver Island. The Western Ribbon Snake, *Thamnophis proximus*, ranges over much of the middle portion of the United States, mostly in the southern half, then further down into Mexico. *Thamnophis radix*, the Plains Garter Snake, is also a resident of the mid-section of the United States, this species being more northerly than southerly, then stretching further north into southern Canada. The Narrowhead Garter Snake, *Thamnophis rufipunctatus*, occurs in two main areas, the first being southeastern Arizona and southwestern New Mexico, the second being in central and western Chihuahua and northern and western Durango in Mexico. The popular Eastern Ribbon Snake, *Thamnophis sauritus*, covers virtually all of the eastern third of the United States and reaches up into Ontario. Finally, the Common Garter Snake, *Thamnophis sirtalis*, can be found over almost all of the United States and Canada, with few exceptions (one of the most notable being its total absence in Arizona).

from a thin strip of central California, running north to south. The Two-striped Garter Snake, *Thamnophis hammondi*, has two disjunct populations, depending on the subspecies. The nominate form occurs in coastal southwestern California, then into northern Baja, while the second subspecies begins much further down in south-central

BEHAVIOR

Most snakes aren't known for their good temper, and in reality, garter

DR. SHERMAN A. MINTON

Thamnophis brachystoma (Shorthead Garter Snake). Primarily a resident of the Allegheny High Plateau, its name is derived from the fact that its head is rarely longer than the width of its neck.

and ribbon snakes shouldn't be either, but the fact is, although they start out rather feisty and "nippy," they will, in time, calm down to the point where they are perfectly the aid of a sand-blaster, and their bites sometimes even break the skin, but they are consequently of no harm to humans.

Garter and ribbon snakes are

Thamnophis sirtalis similis (Bluestripe Garter Snake). Described in 1965 by world *Thamnophis* authority Dr. Douglas Rossman, the Bluestripe Garter Snake is native only to the northwestern coastal region of Florida.

handleable. In the wild, aggressiveness is normal for them. They are quick-moving, alert, and fairly intelligent (for snakes). They are efficient hunters (ribbon snakes will hover over a fish-filled water body with great enthusiasm, darting their heads under the surface at the first sign of a meal) and prolific breeders. If grabbed from the wild, a garter or ribbon snake will very likely bite repeatedly, and even defecate in your hand or release a very musky, awful-smelling scent that seems quite impossible to wash off without generally diurnal, being able to tolerate even the hottest summer days, but occasionally they will become crepuscular, being active more in the early morning hours rather than at dusk. They like to bask and will do so on tree stumps, in grassy fields, or on logs protruding from water. They are excellent swimmers and are often seen gliding across lakes, ponds, and streams, plus they are excellent climbers as well, many specimens being found in bushes and shrubs in both dry locales and, again, near water.

K. H. SWITAK

Thamnophis elegans elegans (Mountain Garter Snake). Garter and ribbon snakes are, for the most part, diurnal creatures. Only during the hottest days will they become crepuscular.

Thamnophis atratus (Santa Cruz Garter Snake). Until only recently, this snake was thought to be nothing more than a subspecies of the Western Aquatic Garter Snake, *Thamnophis couchi.*

R. D. BARTLETT

NATURAL HABITAT

For the most part, the key word with the habitat of *Thamnophis* is *water*. Whatever part of their range you happen to be in, the first place to start looking for them is near any reliable, natural water source. Of course this rule of thumb has its exceptions, but for the most part garter and ribbon snakes depend on water bodies and the ecosystems that surround them for all their ecological needs. Generally speaking, ribbon snakes are slightly more aquatic than garters. Ribbons spend a great deal of their time *in* water whereas garters are often found *near* water, but for the most part, both forms are highly aquatic, so much so that some contemporary herpetologists question whether or not many forms should actually be listed in *Nerodia* with the rest of the water snakes!

Thamnophis habitats can vary from hillsides, meadows, marshes, valleys, mountains, drainage ditches, prairie swales, pine woods, coastal lowlands, depressions, irrigation ditches, backyard gardens, and open fields, to springs, streambeds, and even cemeteries! There are more examples beyond this, of course, but the point has been made. If an interested party wishes to go out and observe wild garter or ribbon snakes, they have a large list of places to choose from.

IDENTIFICATION

The practice of identification in regard to any living creature can be fascinating and fun, but beyond the enjoyable aspect it is also useful to the enthusiast who, at one point in time or another, may *need* to know how to tell one creature from another.

On the generic level, *Thamnophis* can be described as being slender-bodied, having a head that is weakly set off from the rest of the body, having keeled scales, growing to no more than 52 in/130 cm, having a single anal plate, and having light-colored longitudinal stripes that can number from one to three. Patterns

Thamnophis brachystoma (Shorthead Garter Snake). One of the characteristics of the garter and ribbon snakes is a head that is not strongly offset from the rest of the body.

R. D. BARTLETT

DR. SHERMAN A. MINTON

Thamnophis butleri (Butler's Garter Snake). One of the most common characteristics of *Thamnophis* is the stripe on the lower scale rows. It is not present on all of them, but on many.

and colors will of course vary from snake to snake, but the general description given above is accurate enough for the genus.

Given below is a series of brief descriptions illustrating the outstanding characteristics of each of the 16 species of garter and ribbon snakes that occur in the United States and Canada. With these descriptions you should be able to

accurately identify almost any *Thamnophis* that happens to pop up in the commercial market (because, again, those species that occur south of Texas rarely, if ever, show up for sale). So, anytime you go out on a "buying trip" of any kind and have garter or ribbon snakes in mind, bring this book with you. If you wish to further your knowledge into the area of subspecies, there are a number of fine guides you can buy, the most obvious being Dr. Roger Conant and Joseph T. Collins' superb *A Field Guide to Reptiles and Amphibians, Eastern and Central North America*, and its companion volume, *A Field Guide to Western Reptiles and Amphibians*, by Robert C. Stebbins.

SANTA CRUZ GARTER SNAKE
Thamnophis atratus
(Photo on page 13)

Occurring only along the central coast of California (where it overlaps with the Two-striped Garter Snake, *Thamnophis hammondi*, in the southern part of its range), the Santa Cruz Garter Snake is still considered by many to be a subspecies of the Western Aquatic Garter Snake, *Thamnophis couchi*. It is a pretty snake, with a distinctive lemon yellow throat and a beautiful matching vertebral stripe. The base color is a uniform black, or, at the very least, a dark charcoal, and the ventrolateral region is a very pale green.

SHORTHEAD GARTER SNAKE
Thamnophis brachystoma
(Photos on pages 10 & 14)

Growing only to about 18 in/45.7 cm, the Shorthead Garter Snake is

Thamnophis couchi hydrophilus (Oregon Garter Snake). Many herpetologists believe that some, if not all, garter and ribbon snakes belong in the genus *Nerodia*, otherwise known as the water snakes and the Salt Marsh Snakes.

K. H. SWITAK

R. D. BARTLETT

Thamnophis elegans terrestris (Coast Garter Snake). Notice the bright yellow dorsal stripe on this snake. It is a characteristic of the subspecies.

appropriately named—the head is remarkably small, being no longer than the width of the body. The lateral stripes usually occur on rows two and three and are often darkly outlined. Also, this snake has very little in the way of dorsal spotting; it is vague at best.

BUTLER'S GARTER SNAKE
Thamnophis butleri
(Photo on page 15)

Characteristics are weak. The lateral stripes may be orange and the ground color can vary from drab browns to almost a solid black. Stripe usually on row three, extending into rows two and four as well. Spotting may or may not be present. Head very small. Rarely grows over 20 in/ 51 cm.

WESTERN AQUATIC GARTER SNAKE
Thamnophis couchi
(Photo on page 16)

Growing up to about 64 in/160 cm on average, the coloration of this species varies greatly depending on which subspecies you're dealing with. The principal pattern, too, varies greatly. Some distinctive features that are reasonably common include dorsal spotting and a weak dorsal stripe (although apparently in specimens from the central coastal California area the stripe is very clear). Dorsal scales are keeled, in 19 or 21 rows, and the rear chin shields are usually longer than the front pair.

used, the sixth and seventh usually being noticeably enlarged. Also, the dark ground color is often checked with dark markings and there is a mid-dorsal stripe extending from head to tail. Also, the internasals are usually broader than they are long.

GUIDO DINGERKUS

Thamnophis elegans vagrans (Wandering Garter Snake). There reportedly are a number of melanistic specimens of this particular snake located in the Puget Sound region of western Washington and in eastern Oregon.

BLACKNECK GARTER SNAKE
Thamnophis cyrtopsis
(Photos on pages 3 & 39)

Ground color usually a drab green or greenish gray, with a distinct, light-colored (pale white or yellow) mid-dorsal stripe. Belly whitish, white coloring extending up to about the third scale row, and the entire body specked sparingly with black spots. The most prominent characteristic is the one that gives the snake its common name—the distinct black half-oval spots that extend from just behind the head to about three scale rows back.

WESTERN TERRESTRIAL GARTER SNAKE
Thamnophis elegans
(Photos on pages 12, 17, 18, & 38)

This species usually does not grow beyond a length of 43 in/107 cm. A count of eight upper labials can be

MEXICAN GARTER SNAKE
Thamnophis eques
(Photo on page 19)

This snake can be identified by the light-colored (usually greenish) half-moon shaped spots at the corners of the mouth, plus the black blotches behind the head on the top. There are three distinct light-colored stripes, one being mid-dorsal and the others being on the third and forth scale rows. Ground color usually a very dark green with black spotting. Rarely grows over 40 in/100 cm.

GIANT GARTER SNAKE
Thamnophis gigas
(Not illustrated)

Mid-dorsal striping on this species is not particularly strong (usually a pale yellow and often irregular), but the spotting is very dark and neatly

DR. SHERMAN A. MINTON

Thamnophis eques megalops (Northern Mexican Garter Snake). Strongly resembling many of the United States garter snakes, the specimen shown is from Queretaro, Mexico.

arranged in a checkered pattern. *Gigas* gets its common name from the fact that it grows to a length of over 48 in/120 cm, which is considerable for a *Thamnophis*.

TWO-STRIPED GARTER SNAKE
Thamnophis hammondi
(Photo on page 20)

Most easily identified by the fact that there is no mid-dorsal stripe, only those on either side. Ground color can be gray, brown, or olive-green, the dorsum covered with rows of dark spots. Belly pattern and color vary greatly, from yellowish orange to salmon pink with or without light spotting. Rarely grows over 36 in/90 cm.

CHECKERED GARTER SNAKE
Thamnophis marcianus
(Photos on pages 5, 21, & 22)

A most attractive snake, the ground color is usually a drab green, medium yellow, or brown, with a series of regular black, squarish markings. It also has a yellowish mid-dorsal stripe that lightens as it nears the head, almost to the point of being white. Lateral stripes usually begin on only the third scale row, extending to the second as they near the tail. There is also a pair of black blotches just behind the head and light-colored crescents on either corner of the mouth. The dorsolateral region also is flecked with regular black markings.

NORTHWESTERN GARTER SNAKE
Thamnophis ordinoides
(Photo on page 7)

This snake varies greatly in all respects. The ground color can be black, brown, gray, yellowish, tan, or may even have lightly bluish tint, with a mid-dorsal stripe that may either be well-defined or very faint and can be colored in yellow, orange, blue, red, or white. There may or may not even be lateral stripes on the third and fourth rows. Average adult length is around 38 in/95 cm, and the scale rows at mid-body usually number 17. Upper labials are usually seven and the lowers are usually eight or nine. The belly is usually a deciding factor, for although the color there can vary as well (yellow, greenish, brown, black, or ashy gray), there may also be a series of reddish blotches or, at the very least, a reddish tinting, and then perhaps a speckling of small dark markings.

Thamnophis hammondi (Two-striped Garter Snake). So-named because of its two stripes—the broad, uniformly colored stripe that covers the dorsum, and the lighter one(s) on the ventrolateral region.

K. H. SWITAK

MELLA PANZELLA

Thamnophis sauritus sauritus (Eastern Ribbon Snake).

R. D. BARTLETT

***Thamnophis sirtalis sirtalis* (Eastern Garter Snake).** Aberrant pattern with orange coloration.

B. KAHL

Thamnophis sirtalis (Common Garter Snake).

HOUSING GARTER AND RIBBON SNAKES

SIZE OF THE TANK

Since none of the snakes in the genus *Thamnophis* grow over a length of about 50 in/125 cm, the keeper needn't be concerned with the provision of a great amount of captive space. Furthermore, since garter and ribbon snakes seem to have an uncanny adaptability to the confines of captivity, the keeper also needn't be worried that they might one day have to place their stock in something like a greenhouse or an outdoor enclosure, as they might with a large anaconda or python (although let's face it—the garter or ribbon snakes certainly wouldn't mind).

For an adult pair of any *Thamnophis* species, a 20-gallon "long" aquarium is quite sufficient. In dimension, this is roughly 30 in x 1 ft x 1 ft/76 cm x 30 cm x 30 cm. For one adult specimen, a standard 10-gallon aquarium is fine, the dimensions being about 20 in x 1 ft x 10 in/50 cm x 30 cm x 25 cm.

From there you can pretty much calculate whatever space you'll need in regard to what you're keeping. I like to use the formula that

PHOTO COURTESY OF HAGEN.

Finding the correct tank for your garter and/or ribbon snakes certainly won't be a problem. There are many sizes available to the interested enthusiast.

for every additional garter or ribbon snake you keep (of adult size, two young equaling one adult) you should add at least two to four gallons of tank space.

TANK SECURITY

I'll say one thing for garter and ribbon snakes—they sure are crafty little devils. In all the years I've kept herptiles, I can honestly say I've never known any snakes with more cunning than the garters and the ribbons (although the Scarlet Kingsnake, *Lampropeltis elapsoides*, might give them a run for their money).

Thus the keeper of garter and ribbon snakes must give a great deal of attention to tank security. Having a tank that you feel is "good enough" is not, quite frankly, good enough. It must be as tight as...well, tight. The standard quarter-inch hardware cloth tops are rarely adequate, for although they can be locked on the sides with metal curls or clips, the darn *Thamnophis* can slip through the little squares! I learned that the hard way—one of mine apparently tried to "make a break for it" one night using this route and got stuck. The next morning I was greeted by the site of a writhing and wriggling Eastern Garter Snake, *Thamnophis sirtalis sirtalis*, that was suspended off the tank floor, its fat midbody jammed between the rigid wires.

One more horror story, and that should do it—I had only one other case of an escapee garter snake, in this instance a young one that went AWOL in late November, which as

Needless to say, I was delighted to have it back. So, being young and somewhat foolish myself, I set up the animal's old tank again, with only a few refinements in security, and sure enough it escaped again. I found it that time too, but under slightly different circumstances—I opened the door to my snake room unaware that the snake had wedged itself between the bottom of the door and the door's scratch plate. Consequently, I looked down to see a broad scarlet streak running in a left-curve across the

Lighted hoods can be used with many herptiles. They are fairly inexpensive and can be found in most any pet shop.

PHOTO COURTESY OF HAGEN.

anyone else from New Jersey knows can be quite a cold time. Since the animal had been gone for over two weeks and left no forwarding address, I figured it could be written off as a statistic and forgotten about.

Well, the following March I was reminded of how foolish assumptions could be, for the little renegade turned up again in my cellar and looked pretty darn healthy at that. I figured it had hibernated somewhere in the cracks and crevices and sustained itself by taking on the job of Population Control Officer of the tiny invertebrate colony that lived in and around my residence.

linoleum surface and had to take the door off its hinges and actually sand away what was left of my former pet. Nice, huh? Well, that's what happens when snakes get out, so keep it in mind.

Avoid the quarter-inch hardware cloth tops; the holes are too wide for most garter and ribbon snake species. The fine mesh screens are acceptable, but make absolutely sure the tops fit tightly over the tanks. I make a point of saying this because there are a number of tank manufacturers and a number of top manufacturers, and they all design their products slightly different from each other so you will

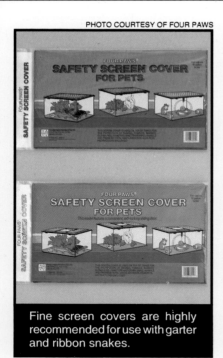

Fine screen covers are highly recommended for use with garter and ribbon snakes.

only buy their products; not all are compatible. It'd be like putting a Yugo engine in a Mack Truck (although I do admit that would probably be pretty funny).

If you have the tools, wood, and skills, you can always build your own tank top but in almost every case such an attempt proves to be a waste of time. There is a small lip that runs along the inside of a glass aquarium's top plastic rim. By measuring the inside of this rim, you can cut a piece of wood accordingly and rest it on this lip, then you can place some screws, nails, or whatever at the edges of your homemade top and use them to hook the clips onto; the other end of the clip will hook onto the outside bottom of the tank's plastic rim. If you're really ambitious, you can build a top that's more like a lid. You will have to do some extra measuring and careful cutting, but in the end you'll have a top that slips over the mouth of the tank like the top on a shoebox.

There are black aluminum clips and shiny steel curls now being manufactured for the purpose of tank security, as well as a number of tops that are made to replace a glass aquarium's upper plastic rim completely. Since it is a matter of your personal choice, it is suggested that you visit you local herp-oriented pet store and make inquiries. Eventually you will find the method of tank security that best suits your wants and needs. But remember, and I can't stress this enough—never underestimate a garter or ribbon snake's ability to escape. They are, plainly and simply, magicians.

CAGE FURNISHINGS

Every snake tank must have its own share of implements on which the snakes can climb, in which to hide, to drink from, etc. In the case of garter and ribbons snakes, these needs are usually minimal.

Cage liners are not only perfectly safe to use with garter and ribbon snakes, but are easy for the keeper to clean, and can be used again and again.

By placing a scenic sheet of one kind or another onto the back of a garter or ribbon snake's tank, you will greatly enhance the tank's visual appeal.

Waterbowls

For most snake species, the waterbowl serves one main purpose—for the snakes to drink from. In the case of garter and ribbon snakes, however, the waterbowl is often a source of food and a place in which to swim. Of course, if you have gone to the trouble of designing a paludarium, then there's no need for a waterbowl at all, but with a terrarium setup, a water body of some sort is necessary.

Therefore, you can't use just any waterbowl, but something more along the lines of a large, shallow tub. Keep in mind that this tub will have to be cleaned and fresh water added every day or two at the least. Many garter and ribbon snake species will take goldfish from their waterbowls, they will swim in it, shed in it, and, of course, defecate in it, so the water gets filthy quick. Plastic is the best material for a waterbowl or watertub to be made from because it's so easy to get clean. Plastic is also light and easy to manipulate.

Rocks

Not only for decoration but also to help a snake begin its shed on, rocks are natural-looking, inexpensive (if you even buy them at all), and reusable. You can build little hiding areas out of rocks but be careful the construction is sturdy; garter and ribbon snakes probably wouldn't survive a cave-in.

For the beginner, there are "start-up" kits that provide all of the basic cage furnishings necessary for garter and ribbon snakes.

Plants

Putting plants, both real and artificial, into a snake tank is usually not a great idea because often the inmates will uproot them through their persistent burrowing or destroy them some other way (breaking the stems, etc.), but in the case of garter and ribbon snakes, adding a few plants into the setup is not necessarily bad. For one thing, none of the *Thamnophis* species are particularly large and thus probably won't cause the flora any real damage. Secondly, most garter and ribbon snakes are not really habitual burrowers so the chances of any plants becoming uprooted are really rather small. Plants add a nice esthetic touch to most any tank and, combined with the proper substrate, will create a beautiful terrarium home for your pets. Furthermore, garter and ribbon snakes like to climb.

Plants, both real and artificial, can be purchased at any number of places, but the shops with the greatest variety are pet shops. Beyond that, a keeper can always visit the local pet store and buy aquatic plants for a paludarium setup. Having a water body filled with natural flora is wonderful to look at, but the snakes might not appreciate it because it makes catching fish a little more challenging! On a positive final note, both real and artificial plants are usually quite inexpensive.

Substrates

The issue of what the best cage bedding to use with any herptile has been hotly debated over the years, but in the case of garter and ribbon snakes the two best choices are probably ordinary potting soil and gravel.

Potting soil is good in the terrarium setup as it allows for plant growth, it is what the inmates are used to in

PHOTO COURTESY OF TETRA/SECOND NATURE.

Artificial plants are, in many ways, very sensible to use with garter and ribbon snakes. They add a nice visual touch to a tank setup and the snakes will enjoy climbing around and hiding behind them.

nature, it is inexpensive, and retains moisture quite well. Since feces will deteriorate into soil so rapidly, the tank will not have to be cleaned as often, either.

If you are setting up the paludarium tank, gravel is perfect. It can be purchased in a wide variety of attractive colors and sizes and is reusable. It also works well with water, as anyone with a fish tank will vouch for. The only problem a keeper may have with gravel is that it is heavy to work with; lugging around a gravel-filled 20-gallon tank during cleaning time is not a prospect you might look forward to. Beyond that small point, gravel is certainly a good choice.

One final suggestion for substrates—paper toweling. When

setting up a generic equivalent to a terrarium tank, the ideal bedding is soft, uncolored paper towels. They are absorbent, inexpensive, easy to clean and replace, and are safe to use with snakes. There is certainly no problem obtaining them, and a roll will last you for weeks or even months, depending on how many setups you've got. Don't underestimate the value of paper towels in any facet of herpetocultural husbandry.

Hiding Places

It is important for all snakes to have a place of privacy. A snake that is constantly exposed will become very stressed and eventually die. Snakes as a general rule aren't terribly social.

There are many ways a keeper can provide a garter or ribbon snake with a hiding place. One, mentioned above, is to pile some rocks together, leaving an open space in the core. Another option is to make a small box from wood. Some keepers choose to leave pieces of bark lying around the tank in the hopes that the snakes will hide under them. Finally, in the generic setups, there is always the plastic hidebox with a hole

Thamnophis sirtalis parietalis (Red-sided Garter Snake). All garter and ribbon snakes need hiding places. Privacy helps reduce a snake's stress level.

RON EVERHART

cut into it. Again, the advantage with plastic is that it can be cleaned thoroughly; wood products will have to be disposed of and replaced, and you may not fancy the idea of running out to your backyard and tearing bark off your trees every week.

Logs and Branches

There is absolutely nothing wrong with decorating a garter or ribbon snake's tank with a few logs or

CLEANING

This subheading really should be included in the chapter on diseases and so forth because cage cleaning is, without question, an affair that is directly related to disease prevention (all good husbandry techniques are, but this one is massively important). The truth is, many captive snakes fall victim to disease because their keepers don't practice cage-cleaning rituals as often as they should or as efficiently as they should.

GUIDO DINGERKUS

Thamnophis elegans vagrans (Wandering Garter Snake). Cleanliness is perhaps the most important aspect of good husbandry. A keeper should be aware that garter and ribbon snakes are very sensitive to filthy surroundings.

branches, but a keeper must remember that wood items are nearly impossible to clean completely and, in the interests of sanitation, all items that have been dirtied and cannot be cleaned should be thrown out.

On the positive side, garter and ribbon snakes will love having a few branches to climb on or a few logs to hide under. If the logs happen to be hollowed out, chances are these will become the snakes's hiding places, but again, there is a sanitary factor to be considered, so be aware.

I will offer a simple step-by-step cage-cleaning method that has been utilized by a number of keepers, including myself, throughout the years, with great success. You can follow it to the letter or modify it here and there to suit your needs, but it is most important that you *do* keep your snakes's tanks clean, because prevention of diseases is a great deal easier than curing them.

1) Remove all the snakes and put them in a secure container. This can be anything suitable, i.e., a plastic shoebox or sweaterbox, a bucket with a locking lid, a large jar, etc.

2) Remove all climate-control items, such as lights, heating apparatus, etc.

3) Remove all items from the tank that are washable and reusable and place them in a bucket. This includes gravel, rocks, plastic waterbowls, and so forth.

4) Remove all disposable items and throw them away, such as paper towels, branches, etc.

5) Remove all plants, if there are any.

6) Fill the now-empty tank with a mixture of warm water, dish soap, and a splash of bleach. The bleach is of course the most powerful cleanser and will effectively destroy most any germs that would otherwise threaten your snakes's health. Scrub the tank clean with a plastic pad (not steel wool, for the glass will get badly scratched), paying special attention to the corners, where the glass meets the plastic rim, and other such subtle spots.

7) Empty out the warm water/soap/bleach mixture and rinse the tank very thoroughly in cold water. Keep rinsing until the effluent is clear and holds no further scent of bleach.

8) Dry the tank thoroughly.

9) Using the same method, now clean all reusable tank items.

10) Now set up the tank again and place the snakes back into it.

11) (optional) Some keepers like to give their snakes a quick bath in order to remove all dried-on crud they may have acquired from being in a dirty tank. If you have a large number of snakes in your collection, then this may be impractical, but it's still a good habit to get into, so if it's

Thamnophis cyrtopsis (Blackneck Garter Snake). Setting up a routine cleaning schedule is something all keepers should do.

K. H. SWITAK

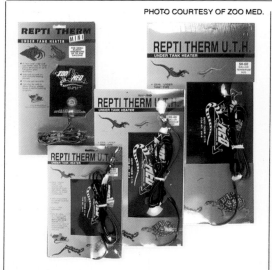

Under-tank heating pads are excellent products for the provision of warmth for garter and ribbon snakes.

feasible then it should be considered. Simply allow the snake(s) to swim around in a basin of warm water for a few moment, rub their bodies with a soft washcloth (needless to say, don't use any soaps), then remove them and dry them thoroughly before finally returning them to their quarters.

Finally, it should be pointed out that there really isn't any need to set a concrete cleaning schedule for yourself; simply tend to the tanks whenever they get dirty. Waterbowls, however, should be cleaned and new water added at least every other day.

TEMPERATURE

The exact daytime temperature for garter and ribbons snakes will vary from species to species depending on what the animal is used to in its natural locale, but for the most part a keeper can maintain any *Thamnophis* at between 75 and 86°F/24 and 30°C. This seems to be a reasonable gradient for all species in question. If you want to get really exact you will have to, again, base your judgment

on where your particular specimen comes from.

There are many ways to provide heat for garter or ribbon snakes. One method is to simply keep them in a heated room. This is called ambient heat and has many advantages. For example, if you have a large number of tanks, you won't have to buy separate heating apparatus for each one. Furthermore, there are now some ceramic heaters that can be purchased at a relatively low price and are really quite efficient.

Although garter and ribbon snakes can tolerate a fairly wide variety of temperatures, it is always a good idea to monitor the temperature at all times.

Another method is the spot lamp. In short, spot lamps heat small areas only (spots). The advantage here is that a snake can come or go to the heated location whenever it feels like, which is a freedom not afforded when a keeper relies on ambient heat. Along the same lines, heated stones provide warmth in only a single area, as do under-tank heating pads. There is also a heat tape product that you simply adhere to the outside of the tank. So, as you can see, there are a number of products for the keeper to choose from, any of which can be obtained, or at the very least ordered, from a pet shop.

LIGHTING

For those of you who have ever kept, or still keep, lizards and turtles, the phrase "full-spectrum lighting" probably means a lot to you. In very simple terms, full-spectrum lighting is an artificial equivalent to sunlight, which captive

Providing correct photoperiod is very important in the keeping of garter and ribbon snakes. Lights like the two shown here are available at most any pet store and will aid a keeper in his or her endeavors.

Correct lighting is essential for captive garter and ribbon snakes. Check you local pet store for the proper equipment you will need.

turtles and lizards need to survive.

Traditionally, snakes have never been known to need this, but recent experiments have shown that those snakes given a regular exposure to full-spectrum lighting have produced better reproduction results. Also, there is probably no harm done to a garter or ribbon snake either way, so why not give full-spectrum lighting a try? I would prescribe a four–to five-hour per day exposure to full-spectrum light, with a further (and overlapping) ten-hour exposure to ordinary lighting. Thus, you would have two timers and two bulbs, the ordinary light turning on at, say, 8:00 a.m., the full-spectrum light turning on at 1:00 p.m., and both switching off at 6:00 p.m.

Full-spectrum bulbs can be purchased at your local pet shop.

SETTING UP THE TANK

For virtually all garter and ribbon snake species, there are basically only two different tank setups a keeper will ever utilize—the terrarium setup, which is mostly land with a small water body, and the paludarium setup, which is half land and half water.

The Terrarium Setup

Take the tank you are planning on using, clean it thoroughly (always start off with a clean tank), then fill it with about a two-inch layer of sterile potting soil. Don't use soil from your backyard or elsewhere because you all garter and ribbon snakes like to swim. There are so many things you can use—a large bowl, a shallow pan (of the kind used in horticulture), a plastic shoebox, etc. Be sure to place it somewhere where you can get to it easily for cleaning purposes because chances are you will be doing it often.

Once you've done all that, set up the climate control items—lights, heating elements, etc. If you want to make things a little easier on yourself, purchase a timer for the

Heated rocks have become very popular in the herpetocultural hobby over the last few years and are perfectly usable with garter and ribbon snakes.

just never know what might be crawling around in it. Potting soil is remarkably inexpensive anyway, so why take a risk?

Once you have bedded the tank, put in the implements—a few rocks, a branch or two for climbing or perhaps some live plants (or artificial ones—make sure they are well-rooted or they will end up on their sides), and perhaps a hidebox. Since you are bothering to set up an actual terrarium in the first place, it is advised that you put in some live plants either way. They are not only an attractive feature all their own, but actually are beneficial to the snakes in many ways.

One thing to remember with garter and ribbon snakes is that you must supply a water body of some sort, and preferably a large one, because lights and a thermostat for the heating equipment. That way, the setup literally becomes self-sustaining.

Finally, place your pets into their new home and let them enjoy.

The Paludarium Setup

Paludarium; that's a pretty interesting word isn't it? In simple terms, as I pointed out before, it denotes a tank that is set up for animals that spend time on both land and water, and many garter and ribbon snakes certainly fall into that category.

Again, wash the tank thoroughly before anything else. During this washing you will also be able to determine whether or not the tank is watertight.

Fill the tank with a layer of gravel

Heat emitters can be used in conjunction with garter and ribbon snakes. These are very efficient in the provision of warmth and can be found in many pet stores.

(pea-sized is good), then pile up more gravel at one end of the tank. This obviously is where the "land mass" will be. Some keepers feel uncomfortable with the idea of amassing such weight into a glass tank; it will, after all, become very difficult to manipulate during cleaning time. If this is your sentiment, an obvious solution is to take a small plastic tub, flip it over, and place it onto the initial gravel bed in the spot where you plan to build the land mass. The air inside the tub will take the place of all those stones but obviously won't add any weight. It is also obvious that the larger the tub, the less space you'll have to fill with gravel.

Now that you've done all

that, you might want to consider setting up a small water filter or some sort. There are so many different styles and types on the market these days that I'm not even going to suggest one; that decision is strictly yours. But keep in mind that the water body probably won't be very high, so don't get a filter that's too tall or else it will be useless.

Fill up the tank with water until the level is about one inch under the line of the land body. Put in a fully submersible water heater if you wish (it is strongly advised) and perhaps a few live aquatic plants. These are so inexpensive and attractive that there really is no reason not to. Then, on the land mass, add in the rocks, hiding area, and so on, and you're done.

GENERIC EQUIVALENT SETUPS

There seems to be a growing contingency of keepers who have apparently made the decision that "looks aren't everything" and throw visual esthetics to the wind in place

If the garter/ribbon snake tank setup you have has a large water body, heating that water body is a perfectly acceptable idea. If the snakes you have like to swim around, they should not do it in cold water.

of setups that are more conservative, clinical, and (hopefully) safer for the snakes. Generic equivalent setups are also easier for the keeper to work with and almost always less expensive to arrange and provide. The ideology includes a bare minimum of furnishings and only the most basic climate control items.

The Terrarium Equivalent

Start with a plastic sweaterbox (which will house one or two adult snakes per), and line it with soft, uncolored paper toweling. Add in a small, shallow, plastic pan and fill it with water, one rock, a plastic container with a hole cut into it for hiding (also bedded with a paper towel), and perhaps one branch, which will be disposed of and replaced weekly. A heating pad under one spot will provide warmth (I like to

put it under the area where the hidebox is), a few small holes drilled into the box's lid will provide ventilation, and a few pieces of tape will provide security. If you are using a glass tank rather than a sweaterbox and want to add in any live plants, simply place them in a separate plastic container, soil and all.

The Paludarium Equivalent

Again, start with a plastic sweaterbox or glass aquarium, fill it with water, add in enough large rocks to make a land body, and a fully submersible heater to warm the water. If you do not use a filter, the water will have to be changed every five days at the least. Also, be sure the land mass is high enough from the water to be truly dry or you will run the risk of your snakes developing skin blisters.

Paludarium setups can be used with many garter and ribbon snake species. Now, paludarium setups can be purchased with all their furnishings and so forth already included.

PHOTO COURTESY OF RIVER TANK

FEEDING GARTER AND RIBBON SNAKES

The keeper of garter and ribbon snakes is truly lucky for many reasons, one being that most of the snakes in the genus *Thamnophis* are voracious feeders. I can't even remember the number of times I have dropped a bunch of goldfish into a large waterbowl only to see the water turn into a mass of swirling ribbon snakes only seconds later.

FOOD ITEMS
Fish

Fish, most particularly feeder goldfish, are probably the food item most often offered to captive garter and ribbon snakes. I mention feeder goldfish most prominently because they are available at most pet stores, are relatively inexpensive, and are taken with great eagerness by garter

JOHN DOMMERS

Thamnophis sirtalis sirtalis (Common Garter Snake). In captivity, providing garter and ribbon snakes with amphibians for food will be, for most keepers, very difficult.

The other nice point about garter and ribbon snake feeding is the fact that most of the food items are easy for the average keeper to acquire. Some snakes, like the kingsnakes (of the genus *Lampropeltis*), for example, have a tendency to eat not only mice, but other snakes as well. Can you imagine trying to supply a hungry snake with a bunch of other snakes every week? Not fun. In the case of the garters and ribbons, however, you not only have a list of items to choose from, but most of them are easy to get your hands on (not to mention inexpensive).

and ribbon snakes.

Many keepers like the idea of buying dead fish from a supermarket, cutting it into small parcels, then freezing the load and drawing from it when necessary. Since garter and ribbon snakes go mostly by scent rather than sight during feeding time, this is not a bad idea. But be careful the fish you buy are not particularly salty, for fish that come from salt water are somewhat alien to garter and ribbon snakes and their systems won't be able to stand the excess salt for very long.

A. V. D. NIEUWENHUIZEN

Thamnophis sirtalis (Common Garter Snake). Amphibians constitute a fairly large part of the diet of wild garter and ribbon snakes.

Thamnophis sirtalis sirtalis (Common Garter Snake). While many garter and ribbon snakes include snakes in their diet, they themsevles are preyed upon by other snakes as well. The snake doing the preying here is a Common Kingsnake, *Lampropeltis getula getula*; a notorious snake-eater.

"Bugs"

I'm using a pretty broad term here because I don't really feel like itemizing the list involved—crickets, slugs, spiders, earthworms, millipedes, etc. Not all of those creatures, nor any of the others that could fall into this category, are truly "insects," but in layman's terms, I'm sure we can call them "bugs," to make things simpler.

Garter and ribbon snakes love bugs. Earthworms are relished by most species, as are slugs and spiders. Crickets have never seemed too popular with *Thamnophis* but they're always worth trying.

Most bugs can be taken right from one's backyard or nearby stretch of woodland. If you don't have any woodland near you, try calling a fisherman's bait shop. If that too is out of the question, try contacting a local herpetological society or check out some classified ads in one of the many herp newsletters of magazines.

Amphibians

You hate to say it, but garter and ribbon snakes certainly love to eat amphibians. Frogs, toads, and salamanders all make great *Thamnophis* food.

As self-respecting

MICHAEL GILROY

Goldfish are offered to captive garter and ribbon snakes probably more often than any other food item. Goldfish are inexpensive, provide good nutrition, and can be obtained in most any pet shop.

don't know for sure. What I do know is that raw beef should not be used as a staple food even if your garter or ribbon snake asks for it by name. Most of the time the meat is too fatty and too far departed from the snake's normal diet. If you can get your specimens to accept raw beef, fine, but only do it on occasion.

herpetoculturists, should we offer them as food? Good question. On the practical side, this happens in the wild, so what's the difference? Furthermore, amphibians make a good meal. The bottom line is, it's purely up to you. The point is, the snakes certainly won't have any problems with it.

Strips of Raw Beef

I have been hearing about garter and ribbon snakes taking strips of raw beef for years, but I have honestly never tried it nor have I ever actually witnessed it. Since *Thamnophis* go so strongly on scent, it is logical to assume you could just rub a goldfish on a small strip of raw beef and have no problem getting a snake to take it, but again, I

PHOTO COURTESY OF FOUR PAWS.

Vitamin sprays are fairly new to the pet market. They can be used with a great number of different reptiles and amphibians and are available at most pet stores that stock herptiles.

Small Mice

There is a surprisingly large number of garter and ribbon snakes (mostly garter snakes) that will eat small mice, and truly, small mice make a great meal for them.

Mice can be obtained from just about any pet store and are reasonably priced. I'll be honest—they usually cost more than crickets or goldfish—but as an occasional supplement they are a superb dietary element.

If you're serious about regularly offering small mice to your garter or ribbon snakes, you can contact one of the many mouse breeders and buy in bulk quantities. Such places can be reached through your local herp society through one of the newsletters or magazines.

Vitamin Supplements

Finally, it is always a good idea to offer any captive reptile a regular dosage of vitamin supplementation at least once every month. Vitamins can be purchased either in powder or liquid form at your local pet store. The vitamins can either be sprinkled on the food items, fed to the food items via their own food (right before being offered to the snakes), or added in conservative quantities to a garter or ribbon snake's water. Regardless of which method you choose, remember not to overdo it, for hypervitaminosis (an over-abundance of vitamins) is just as dangerous as avitaminosis (an under-abundance of same).

A. V. D. NIEUWENHUIZEN

Thamnophis sirtalis (Common Garter Snake). If possible, try to give your garter and/or ribbon snakes an amphibian every once and a while. The fact is, amphibians are very nutritional in spite of the fact that they may be hard to obtain as food items.

BREEDING GARTER AND RIBBON SNAKES

The propagation of captive reptiles has skyrocketed in popularity over the last decade. Depending on the species being kept, everyone from the beginner to the professional can take a shot at herpetoculture and expect reasonable success.

The garter and ribbon snakes are among the easiest serpents to breed—they seem quite willing, most varieties need little in the way of "climatic persuasion," and, perhaps best of all, they bear live young (which means no eggs to deal with). Also, most garter and ribbon snakes have fairly large litters, and the young are pretty easy to feed.

The information given in this chapter will provide you with all the basic knowledge needed to try your hand at *Thamnophis* breeding.

THE FIRST STEP: ARTIFICIAL HIBERNATION

Unless you have captive-bred specimens to start off with, submitting your garter or ribbon snakes to a brief period of artificial hibernation is a must. In the wild, this process triggers the hormones that permit fertility. In short, a wild-caught garter or ribbon snake that has not been hibernated may very well copulate, but the chances of young being produced are small. Although I said tis does not seem to be the case with many captive-raised specimens, out of simple precaution I would hibernate all qualified adults anyway.

Re-creating correct hibernating conditions in the home is not particularly difficult as long as you can provide the necessarytemperature. If you live in

an area where it doesn't get down to about 55°F/13°C for at least six to eight weeks then you may have trouble. Otherwise, the temperature will be provided for you via the kind influence of Mother Nature. It doesn't really matter *where* the snakes hibernate—your garage, basement, attic, etc.—as long as you can access the animals when you need to.

First comes preparation. You cannot hibernate any specimens that aren't in good health. Hibernation is a great strain on a snake, and if it isn't in good shape it may not make it. Make sure those that you plan to hibernate are of good weight and are suffering from no illnesses.

Secondly, the snakes must not eat anything for the last two weeks before hibernation. If there is any food left in the gut, it will ferment and kill them. The reduced temperature of hibernation also reduces the snakes's metabolism and digestion won't take place. To assure that your snakes are "fully cleaned out," stop feeding them two weeks beforehand, as advised above, then, during the last week, give them daily three-hour warm-water baths. These will loosen up and help discharge any remaining wastes.

Now that the snakes are ready, it's time to set up the hibernaculum. Don't let that word intimidate you; it just means "the place where hibernation will take place." It can be anything—a plastic shoebox, a glass aquarium—whatever. It must have a thick layer of soft substrate for the snakes to burrow into (fresh soil is quite good) and a small waterbowl. The container must of course be

Thamnophis sauritus sauritus (Eastern Ribbon Snake). If you look carefully you can see a neonatal Eastern Ribbon Snake squirming near its mother's midbody. To feed this tiny snake you will probably have to give it chopped-up goldfish.

secure (snakes move around even during hibernation and will gladly escape if they can), but it still needs to have a few holes for ventilation.

Drop the snakes's temperature slowly, say, over a four–or five-day period. As I said before, the ideal temperature is around 55°F/13°C, but as low as 50°F/10°C is all right for the temperate-region varieties. When they have reached the prescribed number, cover the "hibernaculum" and don't disturb it further. Bothering your snakes during hibernation is very

dangerous to their health. You should change the water once a week and perhaps look over the animals to see if they're faring all right, but beyond that they should be left alone.

Again, six to eight weeks it the prescribed amount of time garter and ribbon snakes should be hibernated. Any less than that is really taking a risk. In the wild, some species hibernate for half a year!

At the end of the hibernation period, return the snakes to their warm temperature just as slowly as you took them out of it. If you bring them into warmth too quickly you will shock them, and after experiencing the rigors of hibernation this will not do them a bit of good. Don't expect them to start eating right away. It is advised that you keep the tank covered for at least another day or two and allow the snakes to re-orient themselves. Then you can start feeding them again. Also, keep the males and the females separate for the time being.

COPULATION

Once the snakes have returned to their normal routine of eating, sleeping, defecating, and all that, the males and the females can be paired.

The procedure is simple enough— place the female into the male's cage and just wait. It has been said that the best time to do this is just after a female has shed. The theory is that the scent produced from the female's skin after a fresh molt further stimulates a male, but I have always found them to be quite stimulated to begin with! Either way, put the male in with the female and just wait.

If things go according to plan, the first action taken will be the male rubbing his head against the female's coiled-up body, in the hopes of getting her suitably aroused. This can go on for some time, but the norm is about 15 minutes to an hour.

If she is receptive, she will uncoil herself and allow him to ride along her back, at which time the two may begin to twine together and roll around. Then the male will wrap his

Thamnophis sirtalis sirtalis (Eastern Garter Snake). Melanistic and albinistic garter and ribbon snake varieties are available to hobbyists who are willing to spend the time searching out the right dealers. Shown here is a melanistic specimen from Ottowa County, Ohio.

R. ALLAN WINSTEL

Thamnophis sirtalis (Common Garter Snake). It is surprising that more herpetoculturists don't breed albino *Thamnophis*. They are not only very pretty animals, but have large litters, which is a trait that should appeal to any commercial breeder.

JIM MERLI

tail around hers and slip one of his hemipenes into her cloaca. Once they are joined, the sperm is transferred and the deed is done. This final act can take anywhere from 20 minutes to two hours. Any longer than that and the female may get bored and try to move off. Often the male's hemipenis will be too swollen to allow for detachment and he'll just get dragged around. Eventually, however, the two will come apart and that will be that.

Just for the heck of it, try to mate other males with the same female over the next two weeks, and vice-versa, or, at the very least, try mating the same pair a few more times. Afterward, place the female in her own quarters and don't bother her too much until she has given birth. She'll need a very private hidebox during this time (remember—a gravid snake should be submitted to as little stress as possible), raise her heat a little bit, and, if she is willing to take food, give it to her. She'll need all the nutrients she can get.

THE BIRTH OF GARTER AND RIBBON SNAKES

The normal gestation period for garter and ribbon snakes seems to vary from around 95 to 135 days. Toward the end of this period, the keeper should be sure he or she does not handle or otherwise disturb the mother, for she will be under enough stress as it is. In fact, you can actually make life easier for her at this time by covering her cage so she has as much privacy as possible. This is not to say she should not be exposed to her normal photoperiod, but the sight of humans and other normally alien subjects will cause her unnecessary strain.

You should, however, quickly peek into the female's tank once per day to see if any babies have been born. One way to tell if they have, although this is somewhat gross, is to look for bloodied remnants of their embryonic sacs. I have found that many garter and ribbon snakes give birth during the night hours, although I wouldn't say this is a rule (probably just a symptom of captive living), so chances are you won't actually *see* the birth (although if you do get the chance, you are indeed fortunate—it is a fascinating sight). In fact, I have housed more than one large female

Thamnophis without ever even realizing she was gravid, only to find a bloody, gooey mess in her tank and, upon lifting a rock or a waterbowl, found a pack of needle-thin newborns squiggling away as they headed for the next nearest source of cover.

When the young have been born, it is a good idea to remove them from their mother's quarters immediately, for she may eat them. These young, however, can all be housed together because chances are they won't eat each other (like many kingsnakes, *Lampropeltis* sp., for example, might do). No matter how large the litter, a 10-gallon aquarium will provide enough space for the whole crowd. Although some garter and ribbon snakes have been known to give birth to up to 90 young, the average for most is more like somewhere around 20.

Thamnophis sirtalis (Common Garter Snake). Once garter and ribbon snakes have been born, it is best to remove them from the enclosure because there is a chance the mother will eventually eat them.

JIM MERLI

ROBERT T. ZAPPALORTI

Thamnophis sirtalis (Common Garter Snake). Aberrant patterned garter and ribbon snakes are somewhat rare, but they do turn up—this one was found in someone's backyard in Staten Island, New York.

CARE OF YOUNG

A sensible tank setup for newborn *Thamnophis* includes all the climatic details discussed in the housing chapter, plus a reasonable substrate (fresh soil or paper toweling). If you provide rocks and so forth you can expect the little serpents to hide under them constantly.

Feeding neonatal garter and ribbon snakes can be troublesome, but hardly impossible. Some of the more reliable items include tiny tadpoles and guppies, chopped-up goldfish (which can also be frozen and thawed), crickets, spiders, slugs, and earthworms. It should be noted, however, that the latter item, the earthworm, should not be wholly depended upon because studies have shown that it is not nutritionally complete. While a young garter or ribbon snake may be able to survive for a time on a diet of earthworms, the snake will not grow much, if at all, and will eventually die.

Vitamin powders are a good addition to the diet of neonatal *Thamnophis* and are highly recommended, but only in small quantities. Do not utilize vitamin powder during every feeding; once every two weeks is sufficient, and even then only use it sparingly. Remember, a neonatal snake's system is quite delicate and will not be able to tolerate a vitamin overload. Along the same lines, if you can get the snakes to accept it, a little vitamin fluid can be included in their drinking water as well, but again, only in conservative amounts.

If all goes well, a captive-bred *Thamnophis* should be ready to breed within three years. Many keepers have claimed specimens that have bred within 16 months, but this is rare and only accomplished when the snakes are overfed, which is dangerous, irresponsible, and inhumane. Unless you're in some kind of a massive hurry, let the snakes grow normally and they will breed when they're ready.

DISEASES OF GARTER AND RIBBON SNAKES

No matter how hard you try to keep your garter and/or ribbon snakes healthy, chances are one of them will experience some small health problem eventually. Thus, you should be knowledgeable in diagnosing problems while they are in their earliest stages, then have some idea of what to do.

SKIN BLISTERS

Since many of the snakes of the genus *Thamnophis* are highly aquatic, they are susceptible to a number skin ailments, the most common of which is the blister. Many keepers claim that once a garter or ribbon snake, or any other natricine for that matter, falls victim to skin blisters, it is pretty much *in extremis*.

But I have found this to be untrue, at least where the problem has not grown to epidemic proportions. If you have a garter or ribbon snake with a few blisters on its body (which will appear as small swellings that are either clear or filled with a milky white fluid), a treatment you can perform in the home is to pop the blister with a sharp, sterile implement and swab the remaining wound with hydrogen peroxide twice a day for the next week. If the swelling looks like it is coming from under the snake's skin rather than on it, then you need to bring the snake to a veterinarian, as you would if the problem was very extensive, i.e., many blisters scattered all over the animal's body.

JOHN DOMMERS

Thamnophis sirtalis sirtalis (Eastern Garter Snake). When any of your snakes begin a shed phase, be sure they have a water area to bathe in and a rock to begin the shed on.

TICKS

Often a snake will have a tick or two on its body somewhere, but usually you have to look for them. If you find one, don't just grab it and pull (I realize the temptation to do this can be irresistible).

The most sensible procedure is to either light a match, blow it out, and then apply it to the tick (the burning will usually cause the parasite to let go), or cover the tick with a thick dab of petroleum jelly, causing it to suffocate or, again, release itself in the hopes of regaining oxygen. Another solution I have heard of is to dab some sort of alcohol on the tick, but in all honesty I have never tried it. Sounds reasonable, though.

Finally, if all three of the above mentioned techniques don't work,

R. D. BARTLETT

Thamnophis sirtalis sirtalis (Eastern Garter Snake). Spend a moment each week inspecting your snake's head. This is often where the first signs of disease will be most apparent.

take a pair of tweezers and grab the tick as close to the snake's body as you can, then pull very gently. If you pull too hard you run the risk of breaking the tick in half, leaving part of the head in the snake's skin. This will then infect the wound and cause further infection.

Once the tick has been successfully removed, swab the spot with hydrogen peroxide twice a day for one week.

MITES

Mites are a real common problem with captive snakes and they have many origins, but the most common is the inclusion of a new specimen that was already infected. You should make it a habit of checking for mites every few weeks or so. They are nocturnal critters that are so small it'll look like your snake is being attacked by a bunch of printed periods. In order to catch them in the act of, well, I guess you'd call it "miting" (?!), simply turn on the tank's light in the middle of the night and hover over the snake with a magnifying glass.

Once you know you've got them, you have to start the cure. First, place the infected snake(s) into a quarantine tank (this is where the

Terrarium Equivalent Setup is useful—refer to the chapter on housing) and then wash the infested tank out very thoroughly. Take a small piece of insecticidal strip (about a two-inch square ought to suffice), place it in a small container with a bunch of tiny holes drilled into it (a former margarine tub is good), and place the container in with the infested snake(s) for one week. Do not include a waterbowl or, for that matter, *any* body of water at all, with the quarantine tank because the effects of the strip will taint the water, making it unsuitable for drinking.

After the week is up, remove the snakes, clean their quarantine tank, then return them to it for another five days, with a fresh piece of pest strip, to kill off any new mites (hatchlings).

DYSECDYSIS (SHEDDING PROBLEMS)

Most snakes have bad sheds at one time in their life or another; it's nothing to really get alarmed about. Only in extreme cases will any real damage be done, but if you're keeping the snake in your care then the problem shouldn't be allowed to grow this far anyway, right?

Signs of a bad shed are obvious—patches of unshed skin are still adhered to the body. The worst location for stubborn sheddings is of course around the eyes. When a brille (fancy name for an unshed eye cap) refuses to come off, you have a problem. In the worst case scenario, the brille will infect the eye so badly that the snake will eventually lose its vision, at the very least in that one particular eye (often in both). I don't wish to scare you with this illustration; it really doesn't get that bad that often.

What you want to do when a brille is being stubborn is first try to immerse the snake's head in a tub of fairly warm water (warm, not hot) for

a few minutes and then try to peel it off by hand. If your fingers aren't steady enough (this does take nerve and a bit of dexterity) then have someone else do it (a vet or a more experienced keeper). If the warm water treatment doesn't do the trick, try dabbing the brille with mineral oil, waiting about ten minutes for it to soften up, then attempting to peel it off again. If that still doesn't work, then you have a real problem and should bring the snake to a vet before something like our aforementioned Worst Case Scenario becomes a reality.

Other adherent patches of skin can be handled much in the same way—first the hot water both, then, if that doesn't work, a sparing amount of mineral oil, and finally, in desperation, a trip to the vet.

MOUTH ROT (INFECTIOUS STOMATITIS)

One of the more common captive snake ailments, mouth rot can be diagnosed when you begin to see swellings around the snake's mouth, and the snake has trouble closing its jaws completely. The patient will also stop eating altogether (because the act is much too painful) and in later stages the animal will have trouble breathing (although you'd have to get pretty darn close to a garter or ribbon snake in order to her it wheeze!) Mouth rot is usually the result of an inadequate diet—particularly a deficiency of vitamins A and C. Once the infected animal is cured, you will then have to readjust its nutritional picture to assure that the problem does not return. Remember, variety is the key to a good diet with just about any captive herptile.

What can be done to diminish mouth rot? As long as the case you are dealing with is not too severe, a daily swabbing of hydrogen peroxide, povidone-iodine, or sulfamethiazine around all infected areas is a good start, plus don't forget to quarantine the patient immediately. If after a week the infection doesn't begin to improve then you will need to take the animal to a veterinarian for more powerful treatment.

CUTS AND LACERATIONS

Minor wounds can be treated with a daily swabbing of hydrogen peroxide and the snake involved should be placed in a sterile tank with a minumum of furnishings (again, a scaled-down version of The Terrarium Equivalent Setup—and the use of paper toweling as a substrate is a must). With severe cases, however, a keeper may be able to clean the wound and use peroxide, but any type of bandaging or surgery should be done strictly by a professional.

SOME GOOD HEALTH PRACTICES TO GET INTO

To assure that your garter and ribbon snakes always remain in the best of possible health, there are some good husbandry habits you should get yourself into.

1) **Monthly Health Checks.** Once a month, take the time to examine each snake you have under a magnifying glass in bright light. Look for any wounds, blisters, mites, or any of the other problems we've discussed here, plus anything else that you feel is suspicious. This is the best way to catch any illnesses in their earliest stages, because, as you now know, the earlier you catch them the better.

2) **Find a Regular Vet.** There are plenty of excellent veterinarians in practice today and many are capable of handling exotic animals like snakes. Once you come across one

Thamnophis sirtalis (Common Garter Snake). Since garter and ribbon snakes are so aquatic, you should make a point of inspecting their skin very carefully. Blisters left untreated can cause very serious problems later on.

SUSAN C. & HUGH MILLER

Thamnophis sirtalis (Common Garter Snake). Proper handling is essential not only to a garter or ribbon snake's health, but develops a sensible keeper/pet relationship. Snakes that are not handled regularly will be nasty and, consequently, filled with stress.

that you feel is professionally excellent, forge a relationship with that person. It will be beneficial to you, the vet in question, and most of all your snakes, in the future.

3) **Set a Cleaning Schedule and Stick to it.** This is going to take a lot of discipline, especially if you have a large number of setups, but it must be done. Cleaning your pet's cages is the most efficient and effective form of preventive medicine at your disposal. Remember, avoiding a health problem is much easier than dealing with it.

4) **Quarantine All New Members of Your Stock.** A sick snake will cause other snakes to get sick, it's as simple as that. Once you get a new garter or ribbon snake into your home, put it in a quarantine tank for two weeks, inspecting it every couple of days, and see what happens. If there are no signs of ill health, only then should you introduce it to the other members of your collection.

5) **Feed Your Snakes Regularly.** Just because a snake can go a long time without food doesn't mean it should or it wants to. If you can't afford to keep a snake well-fed you shouldn't keep it. Outline a regular feeding schedule and stick to it. Garter and ribbon snakes are almost always very willing feeders, so it's not like you'll have any trouble getting them to eat. Thin snakes not only live poor lives, they are also more susceptible to further disease than those snakes that are hardy and well-fed and, of course, underfeeding your snakes is just plain cruel.

MISCELLANEOUS TOPICS

HANDLING

Anyone who has ever field-collected a garter or ribbon snake will vouch for the fact that the word "feisty" is a very polite way of describing wild specimens. If you ever reach down and grab one off the ground or pull one from a pond or stream, chances are it will empty its bladder into your hand, spray you with an awful-smelling musk, or bite you repeatedly.

This is not to say garter and ribbon snakes necessarily are nasty, just defensive; that's why handling your own specimens regularly is so important. Snakes can be tamed, at least to some degree, but only if they are exposed to human handling on a regular basis. If the specimens you have are already nasty, you might want to consider wearing gloves. Rubber kitchen gloves are the best kind because they not only fit snugly over your hand but snakes hate the taste of them, which of course will teach them not to bite that much quicker.

You'd be amazed how quickly a garter or ribbon snake will become accustomed to human contact. A one-hour handling session three or four times a week for four to six weeks ought to do the trick. (If after that time the animal *still* hasn't calmed down, perhaps you might want to find a way to convert all of its nervous energy into electricity and run all the appliances in your household.)

ACQUIRING GARTER AND RIBBON SNAKES

Since the hobby of herpetology, which I refer to in this book as *herpetoculture*, has become such a sensation, there are a great number of places at the enthusiast's disposal where garter and ribbon snake specimens can be acquired.

The most obvious is at a pet store. Since garters and ribbons have always been quite popular (again, as "beginner's snakes"), it would be hard to find a herptile-stocking pet store that doesn't have them. When shopping around, be sure to check over all animals for signs of ill-health. Check around the eyes, evaluate the snake's weight, inspect the skin. Ask the store owner or manager if you can see it eat (and of course offer to pay for the food). If your instinctive judgment tells you the snake in question is in bad shape, don't buy it.

Professional breeders are another option. Since garter and ribbon snakes are not terribly high-priced animals, only a few select breeders even bother with them. However, if you look hard enough, you can find these people. Most are simply *Thamnophis* fans who breed such stock out of fondness rather than financial desire. There are a number of albino *Thamnophis* species currently being bred, mainly because they can be sold at a high price, but even these are still relatively inexpensive and always very attractive. Breeders can be contacted through society newsletters, journals, and any one of the many herpetological/herpetocultural magazines that are now being published. The only stumbling block to keep in mind here is that most breeders will have to send you your snakes through the mail, and the only legal way to ship snakes (at least in the United States) is by air freight, and the charge for freighting can be rather frightening. Keep that in mind.

Wild collecting is ill-advised regardless of that fact that many garter and ribbon snake species still remain unprotected by any environmental laws. Since garters and ribbons are so easy to breed and raise, it is strongly suggested that captive colonies be built up and used strictly as commercial stock. As the past has taught us (in a very harsh manner), even the most common animal can be reduced to extinction in a relatively short time. Wild-collecting is immoral, unethical, irresponsible, and just plain stupid. It benefits no one, so don't do it.

Finally, you can always join a society in the hopes of getting in touch with others who share your enthusiasm for *Thamnophis* species. By joining societies that are not in your area you can contact people who have access to garter or ribbon snakes you may never otherwise see. You can place classified ads outlining your wants and needs and hopefully find people who have wants and needs of their own. That's when deals are made.

RECORD KEEPING

With the herpetocultural hobby becoming as popular as it is, and through that popularity so many captive-keeping techniques becoming more advanced, complex, and (thankfully) reliable, the need for accurate records is very real.

Even if you aren't thinking of becoming a "serious" keeper, you should still keep records. Of what? Of anything! When your garter or ribbon snake sheds, write it down. If it eats, write it down. Did it throw up a meal? Write it down. This information will very likely be of great value later on, if not to you than to someone else.

I realize most people don't have the time, or even wish to spend the time, brooding over a blank page every time one of their snakes coughs, gags, smiles, sings, or whatever, but lengthy, detailed entries aren't

necessary. Design a condensed language of sorts that you can understand. Use a simple looseleaf notebook or even a pocket cassette recorder. I always favored those big desk calendars. I never put them on my desk but rather on my wall, with a pen taped to a piece of string and left dangling nearby. A typical entry might've read "*T. sirtalis*—2 fish," which obviously meant my Common Garter Snake ate two goldfish that day. It took me perhaps five seconds to jot down the information and I always had it if I ever needed it. Looking back over the dozens of sheets of valuable data I have now accumulated, I'm really happy I bothered to take the time in the first place.

HOW DO GARTER AND RIBBON SNAKES FARE AS PETS?

A major concern that any first-time garter or ribbon snake owner will have, probably even before making his or her initial purchase, is, "Do garter/ribbon snakes do okay in captivity, generally speaking?"

The answer is yes. Snakes in the genus *Thamnophis* are undoubtedly among the hardiest of all captive serpents. They are feisty, alert, fairly intelligent, good eaters, attractive, and, under the proper conditions, will live between five and ten years. The more northerly ranging species are remarkably tolerant of cold weather (certain *Thamnophis* occur well into Canada) and most species overall have only basic captive requirements. Furthermore, virtually anyone can breed them, for this is not a difficult task. Chances are many keepers will have their first captive-breeding successes with garter and/or ribbon snakes. They are excellent pets for any kind of herpetocultural keeper, from the beginner to the professional.

A FEW PROJECTS YOU MIGHT WANT TO CONSIDER

Forming a Society

How come there isn't a Garter and Ribbon Snake Society? There's a society for Green Iguanas, *Iguana iguana*, and a society for the poison frogs, family Dendrobatidae. There's even a society of rat breeders (how frightening), but no society for *Thamnophis*. Some wild enthusiast should start one. At the very least, how about a branch society grown out of a larger host society that focuses on garter and ribbon snakes where most of the members are beginning herpetoculturists? Sort of an "entry level" group for beginning enthusiasts.

Collecting

There are so many different garter and ribbon snake varieties, and many which are available commercially, so why not collect them? Not like stamps or coins, of course, but in a similar spirit. You could go for all the subspecies in a certain species or maybe one representative of each species in a certain geographical zone; there are lots of ways to define what a "collectible group" is (color, habitat, etc.).

Trading

If you have a large number of a single species or subspecies through your captive-breeding efforts, instead of spending the money to buy garter and/or ribbon snakes from other localities you can contact hobbyists who live there and trade with them. Trading herps for others herps will be, believe me, a very popular practice in the near future. As the money angle of this hobby grows more and more notorious, the contingency of people who strictly barter for their stock grows right along with it.

Most bites from non-venomous snakes will only draw blood at best, but any wound should still be treated immediately and the snakes should be handled thereafter (with gloves on) until they become reasonably calm.

W. P. MARA

SUGGESTED READING

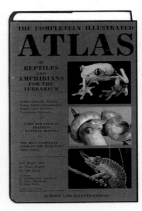

H-1102, 830 pgs, 1800+ photos

TS-165, TWO VOLUME SET, 655 pgs, 1850+ photos

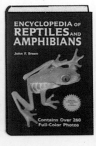

PS-207, 230 pgs, B&W Illus.

H-935, 576 pgs, 260+ photos

PS-876, 384 pgs, 175+ photos

KW-197, 128 pgs, 110+ photos

t.f.h.

PB-126, 64 pgs, 32+ photos

AP-925, 160 pgs, 120+ photos

KW-197, 128 pgs, 110+ photos

J-007, 48 pgs, 25+ photos

TU-015, 64 pgs, 50+ photos

TW-111, 256 pgs, 180+ photos

These and thousands of other animal books have been published by TFH. TFH is the world's largest publisher of animal books. You can find our titles at the same place you bought this one, or write to us for a free catalog.